UNDERWATER

UNDERWATER

poems by

Peter F. Murphy

For Bob!
Thank you for your interest. Great seeing you again & do keep up your own work.

Peter M.
2/16/23

Published by Human Error Publishing
www.humanerrorpublishing.com
paul@humanerrorpublishing.com

Copyright © 2021
by
Human Error Publishing & Peter F. Murphy
All Rights Reserved

ISBN#: 978-1-948521-70-3

Cover design
Cover illustration: Sarah Gutwirth, *Full Fathom Five* (n. d.).
Oil on canvas. 30 x 24 in. By permission of the artist,
sarahgutwirth.com

Cover and contents designed by Theresa Spross,
T. Spross Design, tspross.com

Final design, layout of the book
Peter F. Murphy & Human Error Publishing

For

AGATHA BONITA CRABTREE MURPHY (1911 – 1989)

"AUNT" FLORENCE ESTELL DINGMAN (1909 – 1990),
HER DEAR FRIEND WHO HELPED RAISE ME.

Praise for *Underwater*

Peter F. Murphy's *Underwater* is word drunk in the most soberly playful way–Joycean Americana to the core, following puns and linguistic riffs into byways that veer jauntily from realism to surrealism and back again. *Underwater* revels in the paradoxical wisdoms that are right for our paradoxical time: "With not enough snow the world grows cold." That are right for the paradoxes of our time.

— Andrew Hudgins, author of
After the Lost War and *American Rendering: New and Selected Poems*

What a treat to read Peter F. Murphy's *Underwater,* a cornucopia of portraiture, persona, and wry social commentary. I loved all the oddball characters in these poems, who have chatty liaisons, play out long cons, and crack jokes in surreal scenarios. Murphy makes a feast of puns, misnomers, near-rhymes, and slips of the tongue, resulting in a constant gameplay of language. But make no mistake–underneath the play is a palpable seriousness, and a profound love for the poetic art. Let Murphy's *Underwater* take you for a deep dive.

— Nicky Beer, author of *The Octopus Game*

I love the linguistic nimbleness and wit of these poems. But more than that, I admire the many ways in which they observe the world with a wisdom and love that is flawlessly expressed with a gentle, human touch. Reading this book, I feel guided by a narrator whose gifts originate with a unique life experience which quickly, then, becomes my own–this is how easily *Underwater* invites me into its unassuming, shrewd, and tender point-of-view.

— Daniel Anderson, author of *Drunk in Sunlight*

Peter F. Murphy's poems twist and tumble down the page, riffing on words, images, sounds, and thoughts like a virtuoso saxophonist. Laced with a razor-sharp wit, they glide and swerve, shimmy and stride through their incisive investigations of human nature and the nature of language. Humorous but deeply felt, smart but never pretentious, *Underwater* is a sheer delight.

— Brian Barker, author of *Vanishing Acts*

As William Carlos Williams declared in his great poem "To Elsie," "The pure products of America/go crazy." In *Underwater,* Peter F. Murphy gives us some of these "pure products"—most notably, Farmer Chas in his clawfoot tub. His voice is embedded in a radical American idiom, risky in its playfulness. Williams would heartily applaud. Murphy's poems are sometimes folksy, sometimes bawdy, always lively and intelligent. They are steeped in dialect and puns. A good number constitute virtual primers on how to have fun with rhyme. Beware, anyone who is not among the salt of the earth!

— Ann Neelon, author of *Easter Vigil*

A self-confessed "Formalist," Peter F. Murphy gives the lie to the common assumption that the requirements of form constrain language, that form forces language into tricks and contortions that may not always be "natural" or felicitous. Instead, in Murphy's hands, the constraints of form pressure language into revealing the fractures and slippages, the plastered over skewness of meaning that lie hidden beneath the surfaces of words and their interresonances – revelations that, in turn, enrich (and surprise!) our conception of the world, as encapsulated in language. This, in addition to the already kaleidoscopic insights and queryings Murphy's poems accomplish with any of the wide-ranging topics they take on. This poet admirably works craft into art into wisdom – these poems are the real deal, and should be read with gratitude.

— T. Crunk, author of *Living in the Resurrection*

TABLE OF CONTENTS

ONE

TWO: BURLESQUES

ONE

THE POET'S SPOUSE

Don't ask me. I have no idea
where the ideas
come from. He makes them up.
He must. No one does the kinds
of things he describes. They couldn't and be that kind.

All I can tell you is that he's up
at the crack of dawn
scribbling. What dawns
on him at that ungodly hour
is anybody's guess.

Where his ideas come from, your guess
is as good as mine. He writes for hours,
sometimes all day and on into the night.
I go to sleep at midnight
and he's still up, bent over his journal.

In the morning, before a breakfast
of coffee, black, he's still there writing as fast
as the night before. *It's all in the journals,*
he told me once, *there in black and white.*
Pay attention to the white

spaces. Don't ignore them whatever you do.
And I did. I stole in one night,
the only night
I found him asleep with nothing to write and less to do,
and I studied the lines and the spaces.
It was the spaces,
I have to admit, I found
most confusing. The lines
seemed clear. Short lines
mostly in found

poems, I think.
It was the space, though, that made me think.
I knew about concrete poetry,
the one shaped like a butterfly and one like a snake.
His work didn't snake

around the page at all. His poetry
staggered in lines
sometimes aligned,
frequently ajar,
with space divvied up on the page.

Every page
reminded me of that round, grey jar
in Tennessee. The one on a hill.
Maybe it was more the hill
than the jar. The ground

would be white
by now, even that far south, and white
was the page, grounded
it's true,
in lines more jagged than true.

A Woman

She preferred women to men,
my mother. Short, stocky women
who could protect her in a bar
fight and stand up to a man.

She liked women with money,
generous to a fault,
women who could pay more than their fair share of the tab.

She had rules, my mother:
no hustlers,
no floozies,
no tarts,
no fakes.

She wanted *a woman with class,*
not a pain in the ass.

No up-tight women
or women too-tight.
No slight
women or out-all-night
women.

No ingénues,
no darlings
no dykes.

She was ambivalent about dykes:
flannel shirts,
work boots,
the swagger.

Not ladylike enough for my mother.

She might like *a girl from the streets,*
　　　but not the back alleys,
a woman of town,
　　　just not all over town.

No Girl Friday
over Saturday
for a little something on Sunday,
and stay all the next week.

What she wanted, my mother,
was a woman
to love her
and leave her alone.

Maps of Three Continents

Books lay stacked on the dining-room
table: twelve-step plans, travel guides,
vegetarian cookbooks, and best-sellers
spanning the past decade or two. She

had started them all at one time
or another, bought maps of three
continents, tofu for a stroganoff,
a yoga mat, free weights, and a reading

stand to hold the thousand-page novels
she'd bought on-line. She'd booked flights to Iceland
and Poland, Uruguay and Paraguay,
India and Southeast Asia.

She'd planned a party for sixty,
a soiree for twelve, and a cook-
out with Not-Dogs, three sides, and dessert.
She'd started taking her meds, cut back

on the booze, and stopped pouring salt on her fries.
She went to church when she could, stayed out
of the bars, and volunteered when the cause
was close by. She had no regrets. Her children loved

her. They called now and then, texted when broke,
and stopped by on their way down the shore. She'd
been a good wife, a good mother, a good
friend. The quiet, she knew, would do her some good.

A Third Love Note to Alice

Alas
Alice,
at last
this blast
from the past.

An old pal
your new gal,

one who glares
unawares
when she stares.

More plastic
then elastic,
Alice, this erratic
fanatic,

your friend
you'll defend
'til the end.

A love
long over
by October

Alice, and if not then,
when?

THE CLAW-FOOT TUB

Farmer Chas., while out in his pasture,
decided *"What the Hell,"*
he'd become their pastor.
He could yell
with the best of 'em, scream
admonitions,
interpret their dreams,
and bless their boxes of ammunition.
So what if he didn't know Greek,
had never seen a word of Aramaic,
had no Latin. He could speak
with authority, impose his ethics,
and let them know from the start who was boss.
His gain didn't have to be their loss.

He'd ban TV,
except the 700 club,
praise Adam, not Eve,
and baptize their children in a claw-foot tub.
That would give his operation
some class.
Devotion
would be his watch word. He'd take no sass,
outlaw all doubt,
recite hour-long prayers
to rout out
those who might dare
ask a question or two.
He'd show them who's in charge of the zoo.

He wasn't a stupid man.
He'd been around, seen the sights.
His plan
would be simple. He'd arrive late at night,
seize the pulpit
long before anyone stirred,
and, half-lit,

force them all to their knees in defer-
ence. He'd catch them off guard,
learn of any
untoward
behavior, and in a simple epiphany
demand devotion,
with or without the commotion.

His Bad

He's a good
guy with a good
life, and a good
family that tries to do good

now and then. His wife's a *good*

girl he met at a good
college back when times were good.
He has a good
job making good

money. The business is good,

and he's good
at what he does. His future looks good.
He knows good
from bad, and does good

at a time not known for it's good.

His good-
side usually wins out, and that's good.
It's all good,
his children say, not knowing the bad from the good.

LIABLE

Libel-
ous, the liberal
ran across the court-
yard to the report
of rifles giving a fit-
and-a-start to the official affidavit.

The liberal
was sure he was libel.
He'd sworn to the court
in a formal report
of an affidavit
he'd signed in a fit.

The courtreport-
er thought the affidavit
wouldn't fit
a libel
filed by a liberal,

or a Republican for that matter. The affidavit
stated who was fit,
and the liberal
missed the list. Who was libel
in the report
would be determined by a higher court.

A *full court*
press, the report-
er called it in a short note. The liberal
saw fit
to swear out a new affidavit.
He'd sue for slander this time, not libel.

THIS MAKES FOR PEACE!

for Joan Murray

Do not say today's children don't care,
and tomorrow's won't either.
If today's sun doesn't rise, tomorrow's won't either.
Only your indifference will impair
the quest for calm, not just before the storm,
but long after the last bomb

kills us all. You may impose
your plan for war on the innocent.
It would be like you to declare war on the innocent
while you, ecstatic in the throes
of a sublime ecstasy,
wouldn't know a peace treaty

from a declaration of war. Insensitive
to the needs of a planet stretched
to its limits, a planet so stretched
to its limits its defenders are now active
in their own struggle to remain alive.
When the Earth dies nothing survives.

THE RECRUIT

Jack knew they were in trouble.
Hank, his half-brother,
was buried two floors down in the rubble.
No one moved or would bother
to help them. They were all in denial.
He'll smother,
Jack screamed, *and no matter what,*
you'll answer to me. Jack thought he had clout.

His friends yawned and sat
motionless. They looked astonished.
They thought prat-
falls might work when admonished
by the likes of Jack. The sat-
ellite dish
showed their lieutenant, the regiment's pastor,
going on about the great hereafter,

and they felt relieved.
Hank was still alive
they were sure, and though they grieved
for his misfortune, they knew he'd survive.
They believed,
Jack's friends, that with enough drive
you could conquer the world. They forgot
Hank was up to his neck in dry rot.

Jack went down on one knee.
He pleaded his case,
and said they were all the best company.
Then he sprang to his feet, turned about-face,
and ran for the door. With the tini-
est bit of hope Jack kept apace
with the news on the street.
He refused to admit defeat.

THE AFRICAN DESERT FLY

To flash freeze is to die.

Bugs act stranger than frogs.
Take the African Desert Fly:

      dried in liquid helium
      at four-hundred-fifty degrees

      below zero,
      when warmed and doused

      with water,
      will fly

or the super-cooled, yellow-jacket wasp
queen fawning frostbite at five above.

With not enough snow the world grows cold.

ONE CUP OF COFFEE

If you don't complain
you're not superior.

You couldn't do it better,
have it better,
make it better.

French press isn't perked.

Tick Tock

The tick-born
disease,
tick, tick, ticks. Born
ticking
this time bomb, tick-
tock, ticktock.

WONDER

One might wonder
if the ad for the two-for-one
sale on tuna
had been fine-tuned
by three
specialists in three-
D or four
not-so for-
tunate guys at the five-
and-dime, their high-fives
flashed at a girl of six-
teen. Six
or seven
of them at the Seven-
Eleven ate
a dozen clams, and eight
squid apiece. At nine,
like clock-work, they paid nine-
fifty for ten
more, this time without tentacles.

COMPLICATIONS

Sex, she said, *complicates things.*
The next thing you know there are bells and rings.

I want choices, variety,
one night. You want destiny

with me in the dark.
I want a lark,

not complications.
You want forever with multiplications.

I want to get laid,
maybe get paid.

You want love,
a sign from above.

I want a chance.
You want a slow dance.

I want to play.
You want today,

tomorrow, next month, next year.
I want this day to be dear.

THE LAD, HALF-CLAD

Her lad,
not sad,
like Sir Galahad

in the plaid
from Baghdad.
A rad-lad

ad-
dicted to rad-
ishes and bad

tempers. High on the add-
itions and add-
ons, mad,

as his dad,
a gad-
fly, half-clad

in a style more fad
then dad-
dy's. Glad

she was in the cad-
illac heading back to her pad.
The ad

was clear. She had
seen it for weeks. Monthly *Kad-*
dish readings for men with one gonad.

For Good

The sauce in the Dutch oven began to boil. Pot
and cover alone weigh fifteen
pounds. With the liquid, twenty-five.

Her careful preparations would slow him
down, this time for good. He stumbles
through the patched screen door

matching her sashay
in their Friday-night waltz.
Her dip this time to poach naked shins

and bare toes. Mass, speed, kinetics,
his slide, headfirst into home.

Maybe

She asked if I had a record. I thought
jail time, bail money, lawyer's fees.
She meant a CD,
a signed contract,
live performances with fans.

She asked if I liked pets. I thought,
cats, dogs, a goldfish or two.
She meant a python,
two black-widows, a half-dozen parakeets,
and a gerbil in a large cage with a wheel.

She asked if I wanted a family. I thought
children, sometime, down-the-road, maybe.
She meant her father, three or four siblings,
both sets of grandparents, and a couple
of kids from at least one other marriage.

She asked if I could drive. I thought,
my own car, around town, into the next county
on occasion.
She meant an eighteen-wheeler, cross-country,
overland-and-return.

She asked if I loved her. I thought
forever, without a doubt, in sickness
and in health.
She meant right then, that moment,
maybe on into next week.

ONCE YOU'VE SEEN IT

What do you do
in Belfast
with so much blue,
once you've seen it?

There's nothing special
about having to die.
Rubber bullets
don't bounce.

Three-fifths

Blood relations, proportioned, measure the human
in humanity.
The archaeological dig
unearthed the dignity
of mankind. In tents
under a sun whose intensity
encouraged the media
in its mediocrity,
anthropologists said *No,*
with thunder! to a nobility
that still worshipped Jove.
Our ancestors relied on joviality
aimed to serve
those in charge with a servility

defined much later by Jung. Their animus
toward the animals caused the mutual animosity.
Both sides thought the other dense
and unforgiving. The density
of the night sky gave one gent
a gentility
the others found an effrontery
to their hatred. *If*
only, he said, *we could ban*
the banality
that racism gives us street-cred,
and embrace with credulity
the gravity
of ideas meant to send us all to an early grave.

Four AM

She wondered what he meant by *shabby*.
She liked his gestures and their intimacy,
though not so much his muddy
boots, his tangled hair, and his eyes fiery
like her dog's, a mangy
mutt, half-starved, and lame. A canopy
their camp, security
in a bounteous bevy
of unkempt women known to be easy.

At first she thought it was *sleazy*,
he'd yelled from the Humvee,
meant to shatter the sanctity
of the places she went to be happy.
The mules she drove there with a *gee-*
and-a-haw, a mastery
she had been told a lady
would never obtain. *In an emergency,*
he acquiesced, *maybe*.

THE GARDEN

Naked,
Adam
amazed
his kin
with the snake.

Young Eve faked
it. Naïve,
she believed
the snake
would make her eat cake.

The snake
loved the tree
and Eve in its branches. She
felt half-baked
that close to the lake,

her, the two hens, and their drake.
Adam was dazed,
done-in, spaced-
out, a man in need of a break.
Eve took her cue from the snake.

DIRTY FACE, RIPPLE & WILD

for Robert Creeley

The first used to chew
& never wipe his chin.

The second shot
his leg about off
going over a fence.

The third drank a lot
and raised hell.

Dirty Face married
and raised a big family,
but kept not
wiping his chin.

Ripple had a peg leg
carved to his specs
in the shape of a penis.

He joked
his middle leg
was twice as big.

Wild stopped drinking
and died of a stroke.

They're buried together now
in the blackberry patch miles
back in the woods.

OTHERS

for Edna St. Vincent Millay

All the herbs arrived in excellent
condition. When do you sail?
There are things to remember: holiday

fragments, frequent
holes in your stockings,
and the square deal in composition.

Three millimeters below sea level
men work where others are others, too.

UNDERWATER

Jimmy tipped the Merc over the transom
almost following it in. Precautions
seeped out with the smell of closing-time.

It's not the water, it's the air
that makes traps rust. In the river
they'd be fine. The minute they break
the surface, they start to rot.

We traced his line all morning in the hope
of a beaver to nail round for a coat
or a mink we'd stretch skinny on a board
rubbed smooth. Bounty to cover bar
tabs and calm alimony's rage.

Jimmy curved the spring over the trap's blunt
jaws past a trigger filed thin. He cracked black
ice and placed the trap in a run among the weeds.
His fingers half-frozen, he never tripped the pan.

The stop loss holds their head
back so they can't chew off a leg.

Muskrat saddles fried in chicken gizzards
would be payment enough.

BEREFT

I saw this and this and this.
What, what, what she had to insist,
knowing the why and the how
and the when. Tell her by noon tomorrow.

So I did, with the details
demanded of short tales
told now and then, once or twice,
a story not long on advice.

*

The legless woman crawled the kilometer
for a crust of bread with no butter
from a commandant peeing next
to his truck. Bereft

he was, with his nose blown away,
and wondering what the delay
was this time. She wailed
to see him impaled,

lifted both arms, and rolled over
to wave a revolver
at the back of his head. Her petard,
a large shard

stained bright red,
like the rag tied tight round his head.
The knot he had learned while at sea.
She wondered how, with her vision, she would see

a spot so small and blood-smeared. She closed her one eye,
nodded a silent goodbye,
and gazed out across the terrain.
He flinched once to the beat of a migraine.

Knowing You As I Do

What would you say
to a beast or a slave
if you needed a ride

into town? Would you wave
to the slave and ask the beast to stay,
or would you threaten them both with their hide?

Knowing you as I do, I'd say you'd deride
the pair not the one, in a foray
only you could devise. Belied

by stories of your own making, lies to portray
you as heroic in an enclave
whose hope only you could abide.

At a minimum, the wait would subside.

FOR JAMES TURRELL, ON VIEWING AT DAWN , "SKYSPACE,"
CHESTNUT HILL FRIENDS MEETING HOUSE, JULY 2, 2017

Yes, and the war.
What war?
We're not at war.

The war of the worlds,
the world at war,
both World Wars.

The Persian Wars,
the Punic Wars,
the Opium Wars,

the Napoleonic Wars.
The Trojan War,
the Peloponnesian War,

the War
of the Spanish Succession. The Six-Days War,
the Thirty Years War,

the Hundred Years War,
the 780-year war
(The Reconquista, 711-1492).

King Philips War,
the War
of the Roses, the Crimean War,

the French and Indian War,
the Mexican-American War,
the Spanish Civil War.

The War
of 1812, the Boer War.
Vietnam, Granada, Iraq, Afghanistan, the Korean war.

Oh, that war,
those wars,
the war.

To Maidenhood

Attired in anonymity,
the kind nurse sang a hymn to the virgins.

Midnight,
she pondered,
pausing
to count on her fingers.

Eight hours from now.

THE TELL-TALE TOUCH

for Sarah

When our lips speak together,
labile the pleasure,
the tell-tale touch
on the tip of your tongue.

Labial, you correct me,
the pleasure's all mine.

They Said

They said you'd win,
that you were a winner.

They said you'd go far,
fly high, and go farther

then any of the rest of us. They said you were brilliant,
not like a diamond, with a brilliance

more divine. They said you were gifted,
and those gifts

you'd share. They said you were generous,
sui generis,

I think one of them said. They said you were good.
Not a goody-

two-shoes. A man.
Not too manly.

A humble
man, with an inkling to hum.

They said you had ability,
with a capability

never before seen. Others said you were stupid,
and that your stupidity

ran way back, generations,
far into the past. The rations,

they said, made you a smarty-
pants who thought you were smarter

then the rest, and too good for us all.
They were known to think small.

BALLYCURRAGH

for James Joyce

Where there wasn't a horse begat,
or a man shaved
or hen went off with the cock of another man's hen yard,
or a boar gelded,
or a priest drunk,
since Adam was three months old.

Ah, it's a slow place,
and a dull place,
and no part of the world.

A CRIMP IN HER STYLE

Her first choice was not the Betty
Ford Clinic. She wouldn't buckle
under pressure or slump
into the doldrums. She tried not to grunt
when her argument started to crumble,
and her husband said a cobbler

was all she needed to cobble
her life back together. Betty,
for that was her name, didn't crumble
when her monogrammed buckle,
designed she was sure to make women grunt,
put her emotional life in a slump.

Her husband lived deep in his own slump.
His answer was always a cobbler,
for any problem: for a grunt
sighed at night, to Betty
in slacks with a belt and no buckle.
She needed one made of silver, guaranteed not to crumble.

Rise up, breath deep, and don't crumble,
he barked. *They want you defeated, in a slump.*
They love to see people buckle.
You'll need to cobble
together a plan, a way to save Betty
from a laugh you might mistake for a grunt.

Faced first with a cough, then a grunt,
her husband began to crumble.
He sighed when he spoke of Betty,
tried to stand tall, not slump,
and mentioned, again, the need for a cobbler.
One more hole in your belt will loosen the buckle.

What he missed was the size of the buckle.
Betty tried to explain between grunts,
yelling *to hell with the cobbler,*
I'm after the blackberry crumble.
Her husband was in a terrible slump.
He'd missed the apple brown betty.

Betty sighed. *The belt buckle isn't the problem. I'll crumble*
if I grunt or not. I'm in a slump,
and no cobbler and his awl will fix Betty.

CHARLOTTE

Charlotte,
this is going to be short.
Short, Charlotte,
like your stint
with the pimp,
that shrimp
with a limp
and gold teeth.

Your hot,
Charlotte,
but
you're not a whore.
You're the bore
I adore
while on shore.
Don't seethe,

Charlotte.
It's your lot
to be apart
from the crew.
What else could I do?
You've never been true.
You
think it's beneath

you Charlotte,
to drop out,
smoke pot,
go crazy.
You're not lazy.
You like Zee-Zee
Top, *a snazzy*
band that makes you breathe

heavy with the thought
your heart
could appear
somewhere near
or afar. Be sincere,
dear,
when you reappear.
Stand up for what you believe.

Don't be a chicken, Charlotte,
a pullet
or a mullet,
a bottom-feeder, indiscriminate
in action and sentiment.
Repent
Charlotte, relent,
and give us all some much-needed relief.

SOLUTIONS

Coca-Cola her universal
solution: an upset stomach,
bugs on the windshield, rusted bolts
or a BBQ sauce in need of sweetener,
all could be cured with a splash of coke.

When someone pointed out the obvious,
oxidized nuts and stomach linings,
she refused to see the connection
adding another shot of rum
to an already laced cocktail. More

ice would only dilute it,
and the coke was no more than a chaser.

YAK, YAK, YAK

I.

He tried to snake
her, once, in the back seat of her father's Falcon.

II.

She went ape
when he pawed her beaver,
and snagged his pecker
in the fly
of her shorts. She wormed

her way out, but the memory dogged
her for years. She bugged
his room, batted
her eyes, fished
in his pockets for change, and squirreled

away ten-dollar bills when she could. Cowed
by his monkey-
shines, she lionized
him. He'd never rat
you out. He'd clam-

up first. He'd horsed
around, hogged
the hootch, wolfed
his cookies on occasion, and swallowed
more shots than he should. He'd hawked

tickets at the circus, been cold-cocked
by a sucker-
punch, and slugged
a skunk
who used *swan*
without an object to declare a surprise. A shark,

he crowed
to his friends when goosed
by a yak
on the lam.

III.

She couldn't bear
it when he played possum.
She knew he was frogging
around, trying to seal
the deal, taking his foe for a trout.

IV.

She started to flounder
when, mousy
as usual, she chickened-
out, out-foxed
by an eagle-
eyed rattler
in a bear
hug. She'd been buffaloed
by a pig
who catted
around, an ass
who knew when to duck.

AT'S ALL

At's all
asshole,

your intermittent
imprisonment

has left you vulnerable,
not venerable.

Incontrovertible
evidence puts you in a convertible

heading south. The official version
mentions a virgin,

and short verses
you wrote on a poster of Sugar Ray vs.

some dude's name they couldn't make out. It looked Finnish.
They weren't sure. You're finished,

that's for sure. The virus
alone you tried to wire us

made the senior statesmen
furious. They want a clear statement

of why you want to dilate
eyes of those who live long and die late.

What do you expect to learn? Your answer,
though spare, needs to exceed an ampersand.

Voyage VII

(for Hart Crane)

> *Just as you stand and lean on the rail, yet hurry with the*
> *swift current, I stood yet was hurried . . .*

> Walt Whitman
> "Crossing Brooklyn Ferry"

How curious you are, bent from the foam
and the waves. Captain of the doubloon isle,
brine-eyed Merman, all night the water combs
you with black insolence.

Your dream or Uncle John's?

Beyond the dykes, water-ways run
ribboned and still. Simple ripples drift
eye-level in muscular song.

Some men take their liquor slow – and count.
Unfettered the sea is cruel.

I love you, O you entirely possess me.

Where twelfth-month seagulls stroke and float.
Where, on a dusty shore, Melville's weaver-
    god, deafened for life, sings tide-less spells
        to the dice of drowned bones.
Where the thick-stemm'd steamboats leap and converge.

The Father of Waters, slight,
alights

by nighest name,
by clear loud voices,
by the river
approaching and passing.

Your eyes pressed black against the prow,
view voyages in fresh ruffles of surf. Cutty Sark,
your white sail'd clipper moored to
your first choice in scotch.

Your soul, deep like the rivers,
swims ancient, dusky rivers,
bloody at dawn.

Abandoned in mists of amorous madness,
your sailors, pent-up, sit
upright, astride scallop-edged spars.
The *S. S. Ala* – Antwerp –

now remember kid, put me out at three. She sails on time.

                                        . . . let the waves rear
like flat lily petals on the sea's white
throat. This transitional place imagined again.

PATIENCE

The Mayflies
    arrive in July,
        to fructify
           and die.

        Their carcasses,
           clay-gray,
              cascade
                for a day.

          Silken
             skeletons
                descend,
                  spent.

.

SMOKING OR NON-SMOKING

Hell is hot, sayeth the Lord. We don't deserve anything.
You can pray until your knees turn blue.
Will your eternal home be smoking or non-smoking?

You may wish you deserved something.
Don't worry, Moses was a basket case, too.
Will your eternal home be smoking or non-smoking?

Keep both feet on the ground and avoid dancing.
Never wear those funny shoes, and nary a tutu.
Hell is hot, sayeth the Lord. We don't deserve anything.

You can dream of a destination wedding,
both of you mindful and in the mood,
but will your eternal home be smoking or non-smoking?

No drinking, no petting, and no French kissing.
One false step and we'll bid you adieu.
Hell is hot, sayeth the Lord. We don't deserve anything.

Forget evolution, gravity, black holes, and String
Theory. No science and no Yahoo!
Remember, Hell is hot and we don't deserve anything.
Will your eternal home be smoking or non-smoking?

REBIRTH

Born between melancholy and mirth,
she laughed 'till she cried.
She made love, gave birth,
and in the end defied
the future her times prescribed.

An infant when her father died,
she sought in later years to unearth
his history and renew the family pride.
She knew of his girth,
and the hedge-stone hearth

at his home on the firth
where he chose to reside.
There where he'd defended his worth
in a style she thought best to descry.
She'd tell the truth, avoid even the smallest white lie,

and provide an endless supply
of anecdote and tall tale. There would be no dearth
of detail. When she was a child,
living near Perth,
she'd learned to prevaricate. She could imply

the half-truth, and decry
the stories of his military service.
She'd keep it unspecified,
delivered with a verve
she'd challenge anyone to defy.

BOTH SIDES

Everything has two sides. Dishes
in the sink, the battle-royal
last night, the news on late-
night TV. Even the stamps
for the postcards could be licked on both sides.

The other had more to do with balance,
of seeing both sides, appreciating
the other point
of view,
than with cultural difference

or someone not yourself.
There are two sides to every argument.
You're not always right just because
you are loudest. Listen to the other
person. You might learn something. Shh.

An Epitaph for Mortal Folk

for Elizabeth Bishop

Tomorrow she sets out for Castine
with four angry guinea pigs. A nice, big,
hearty Maine girl who fell in among thieves.

She embroidered an epitaph for mortal
folk, her invocation to youth. The appeal
an earnest suit, unkind, tearful.

She watched her hair turn gray
practically before her eyes,
and her brother

hitched to a plow when the last ox died.
The loneliest person who ever lived,
she knew all the tugs by name.

The Voices we Hear

Protestants are quiet.
They're passive, compliant.

They dislike dispute
and dissent, the disrepute-

able, but not the deplorable. They're conformists.
They don't like loud voices. Apologists

with prayers
for the unfortunate, more nay-sayers

than yea-sayers, good Protestants
proselytize. Like prostitutes

they pander
their wares. They meander

through chapter
and verse while awaiting the rapture.

Protestants protest too little.
They dribble

when they should shoot.

To the Modernists: A Cento

While my hair was still cut straight across my forehead
Jove in the clouds had his inhuman birth.
The goat coughs at night in the field overhead
for an old bitch gone in the teeth.

Patriarchal poetry one two three.
I, too, dislike it: there are things that are important beyond all this
    fiddle.
Whirl up, sea –
until our blood, commingling, virginal.

The trees are in their autumn beauty.
White desire, empty, a single stem,
you have the ground sense necessary.
Poetry is the supreme fiction, Madame.

We were very tired, we were very merry.
There is nothing more to say,
while to its alien gods I bend my knee.
One of those white summer days

in leaves no step had trodden black.
To learn about not launching out too soon
at the violet hour, when the eyes and back
under the brown fog of a winter noon

is to is no is to is no gain.
A man and a woman and a blackbird,
among the rain:
tendons, muscles shattered, outer husk dismembered.

He moves in darkness, as it seems to me,
like a patient etherized upon the table
with a wicked pack of cards. *Here,* said she,
by the road to the contagious hospital,

a cluster, flower by flower.
The work of hunters is another thing
and just as human as they ever were.
It was evening all afternoon.

Saffron from the fringe of the earth,
a black cloud full of storms too hot for keeping.
The mouse's limp tail hanging like a shoelace from its mouth.
As of the great wind howling

where wine is spilled on promiscuous lips
there was such speed in her little body.
She rested on a log and tossed the fresh chips:
me you – you – me.

COUPLETS CONCERNING MARGARET

for Donald Justice

Have I not met you, merry, at the farmer's market,
Margaret?

You in a teal-green negligee,
neon in the intensity of your negligence.

You were en route to the rapture,
a respite, the original rupture.

Ascribed to the sacred,
it made me squirrely and scared.

I was willing to repent, atone,
in my own home, alone.

You thought me depraved, a deist,
and threatened a cease-and-desist

order. All those miserable missives,
the mimes and the mimics,

in chorus, harmonious, united.
I thought we'd agreed to untied.

AL'S VACATION

for Lorine Niedecker

You once spoke to me of rocks.
Someone there?
Is it Will Petersen?
I wonder if Bosho
is still used in speech for Bon

Jour! Indian, French, British –.
Only like a ton of rock,
the country is part
Lake Superior agate, part jaspar.
Geologic –

the Thompsonite region,
sending stone costs skyward.
They weigh up.
I bought,
at little or nothing,

a carnelian (Oh, that color),
from Uruguay,
and a sodilite
from Canada.
Thin, circling

lines, a wide-
orange band,
the Northwest Passage
to the Orient
has its Bosho.

Riff on E

Early
earls
entered
Eden
ecstatic.
Everywhere
everyone
ended
elegant-
edged

ears.
Elephant
eras
elapsed.
Equilibrium-
eating
egrets,
enthusiastic,
elongated
Eric.

Elevated
elms,
evergreens,
embossed
events.
Evaporated
ecstasy
emitted
ewes'
everdown.

Estimated
evasions
elastic.
Exuberance
erroneous.
Enemies'
enemas
even
evacuated
enameled

entropies.
Entertaining
ecoli
effervescent,
eloquent.
Edsels
extended
executive
excellence
exacto.

SHALL WE

Shall we shower
together,
my dear,
you in the front,
me in the rear,
and the soap
on a rope
'round my neck?

To the Books I Left Behind

Had I
read you.
I don't know,
had I?

DIVINE DESIGN

A race of creatures
neither
human
nor divine
differ
in scope and design.

NOTICE OF NONDISCRIMINATION

Atencion
Chu Y
Paunawa
Atansyon
Attention
Uwaga
Atencao
Attenzione
Achtung
Mloog Zoo
Perhatian
Dikkat
Merk
Atencio
Nrubama
Akiyesi
Ni songen mwohmw ohte
E kaulona mai
Maando
Atension
Dii baa ako' ninimzindoo
Anumpa Pa Pisah
Digniin
Xiyyeeffannaa
Pakdaar
Kujdes
Obavjestenje
Fa'aaliga
Lale
Atentie
Mie Auchea
Tokanga'i Mai
Atensyon
Icitonderwa
Kumbuka

Variations on a Line from Frost

I feel as if it couldn't hurt you
(who are no fool),
and may even do
you some good.

I want you
to see young
what a thing
it is, amusing,

edifying
even, this terrible thing.
You, alone,
of anyone.

THE PETER PRINCIPLE

Your poems peter-out, the editor
wrote in a short note.
What could I say?

*They get murky
and, to be frank,
Francis, need substitutions.*

I thought of the Peter-principle,
Murphy's Law, the editor,
and I wondered,
who had risen too rapidly
and whose luck had run out.

ADVICE FOR A YOUNG POET

from James Merrill

The point is to feel
your feeling,
in the presence of something
in the "outside world"

– in a tree,
a portrait,
the hood of a car,
an article about a new scientific discovery

– which will reflect
your heightened state of mind back
to you.
You will not have to say I.

THE POET'S ACOLYTE

When Francis Murphy sought an acolyte,
he went to town at dawn and stayed all night.
He decided early to seek a man
whose last name was anything but Murphy.
He was surprised to find a young woman
they called Murray, whose poetry
even the great Francis Murphy
had to admit was brand-new and not worn
to a frazzle. Murphy had sworn
more than once on more than a stack of Bibles
that he would bestow on any student,
even those associated with the rabble,
his skill at writing lines both permanent
and sonorous. His predicament,

when he awoke the next day rather late,
came with Murray, barely awake,
and asking for her first cup of coffee.
She had a pen in her hand and a pad
by her side as she squirmed to get comfy.
Her teeth chattered between lips a faint red
as she pondered the room, the man, and the bed.
Frozen, our Ms. Murray, she had made peace
with the devil, and felt appeased
in spite of the draft. A poet in bed,
whether young, middle-aged or old,
could deliver tea that was sweet, corn bread,
some jam, homemade, and warmth against the cold
she felt to her toes. Murphy looked up, rolled

over, and smiled. Murray felt bad.
She was thinking of the sweet, strapping lad
she had left last night at the bar.
She adjusted the specs on her nose
and tried to be there, not somewhere afar.
Murphy said little. He arose
from the bed with a giggle and strove

to act like the poet she needed. Sly
he was, with a line he knew would belie
her assumptions about poets as liars.
Murray smiled too, kept quiet and laid back
pulling the covers up to her neck for a collar.
Murphy made tea, warmed up wheat toast for a snack,
and rehearsed lines to rhyme rack with attack.

TWO: Burlesques

Blown Apart

Late in the month, when he was off his
meds and struggling through contests
not of his own making, she had become pregnant.
He felt at once the oldster
he was. They were at the seashore.
She loved the Moderns, the "effete

aesthete,"
as she liked to call them. They met in his office,
so far out they could see shore
only at night. She looked for contents,
not contexts, when he waved a rhinestone holster
at her head. He invited her to, maybe, come pregnant

to a party he knew about in two Datsuns
jacked up on oak blocks. The ball bearings
were long gone, stolen by this guy
who had come once before.
Her favorite was Eliot.
She was blown apart

by *Four Quartets*, though Bonaparte
could have received mention. Dachshunds
ambled about, it seemed just for the hell of it,
in collars of link chain, bare rings,
and rope braided taut like beef or
pork jerky. The sky

covered over in rain. No body
was ever found. A rival
inflicted reverse peristalsis,
and then read the *Hadran*
in a room no Moor
had seen. Only the rich, a magnate

or two, to act as a magnet
for their well-heeled friends. You couldn't be a nobody.
They'd tried that before and no more.
The recent arrival
of some guy with a hard-on
for an alchemist named Parcelsus

brought them to a plane surface.   She would want a
spa with full service,   a masseuse named Wanda,
and her pelvis aligned with her cervix.   Wanna, wanna, wanna.

Seasons

Lee had heard carbolic acid
heated over pure quartz
makes adults livid,
and prevents a masturbator
from pleading innocent.
He wanted plain, everyday justice.

Sally would take hers with crushed ice,
like El Cid
in the movie. Insolent,
her response to the Crown. They'd drunk quarts
of bad ale to the master baker,
and declared how great a life he'd lived.

Sally opted out for the leisure,
and felt secure
with the .38 under her pillow. Lee was erect
no matter the season,
and raised hell, alas,
to make history erase-able.

An irascible
cut-throat, Lee, sure
had the best alias.
The sea cure
he'd found near the sea. Sons
and daughters would come later. He'd been a wreck.

With a smaller dosage in Cuba he ate her
for dessert. Never a cross word
from that day forward. Partially,
though not probably, the meteor
will burst through the cellophane
holding it away from south Texas.

Sally had read all the texts
and designed the incubator
to monitor her cell phone.
In seconds she'd finished the *Times* crossword
puzzle, literally at meteoric
speed. Flat-leaf parsley,

she said, kept her sane
You know the sayin':
loaned by Sinn

that week on the Seine.
if it weren't for a sein
Fein, we'd all have the sin.

Due By

She lacked the interest, he the impetus.
She'd been puffin with his pumpin'
for what seemed like a century.
He drank blackstrap
molasses, warm with fake flora,
in a pint of white tea. By her accounting,

only a Count Ting
could cure his impotence.
She'd had heard south Florida
was the place for baked pumpkin,
and a diet rich in iron.
He had been the neighborhood sentry.

She helped him get his rocks off,
in her despair.
They headed west on a Boeing
707. *It's the love lines sis,*
he blurted out when the plane left the ground. Cunnilingus
was now out of the question, and the threat of a bullet

wouldn't change anything. Dinner was brief. They could boil it,
fry it or brine it in rock salt.
The choices were few. A cunning linguist
talked about his pair,
not hers, and the loveliness
of the split in bowling.

She'd visit the Acropolis
where infamous and notable
warriors could be seen trying to drag-and-
drop their enemy. He could care less.
The check was due by
the end of the month. Her verses

would be out in the fall. It was a friendly collection. No versus
anything. The poems on the apocalypse
came straight from their trip to Dubai.
Note, a bull
horn on the fritz made her careless
when, out of the ground, all aflame, came the dragon.

A tromp l'oeil,   a bit skewed,
on the wonders of Trump Oil.   It skewered
the Trump ploy,   and no one got screwed.

A Wreck

If there was one thing he knew it was cattle. Pillar-
to-post, his life, a story that made her livid.
He was such a selfish
piece-of-shit. He wanted brassier
at home or
quiet behind the plate. *Psst,*

she whispered, pissed
off at the caterpillar
who had strung her along. Homer
was no help, having lived
so long ago. She'd use a brazier
to cook the fresh shellfish,

and try hard to not make a wreck
of the place. It's all she had. Been
around the block more than once, addicted
to a sailor who owned his own sextant
and could tell down from up. An Aztec,
he was an irascible

old-bird who insisted his history was not erasable.
She didn't care, as long as he could still get erect.
She had her doubts. As tech
manager he was already a has been,
and his jazz sextet
fizzled out when a dick, Ted,

tried to sell him a jar
glazed with an illegal coral.
Art made by a guy in solitary.
Apart or together
they loved a tasty pesto,
and planned the much-needed alteration

to his jeans. When, in an altercation
in Tulsa he left the window ajar,
she leapt from the bed presto-
chango singing a carol
she'd heard on the news. They'd come to gather
in this sultry

swamp, and got busted   for pot they never owned.
Bust Ed,   if you need someone. He's owed
a trip on the bus. Ted,   for you, he'll write a short ode.

Dis Close

The great Protestant Protector
bled from a new wound
won at war. No one could disclose
where the battle would be fought or where the weapons are. A
shrewd guess
was all they wanted. Bring back the comedians,

the Arcadians or the Canadians,
someone to protect her.
They'd give her permanent guest
status, and credit her for the wool she'd wound
round his wrists. The immediate area
was closed off being dis close

to a greenhouse packed with cannabis.
Her Jungian therapist
worked in teams of ten. His highly trained crews are
prepared for anything. Enemies
of all kinds, the nicest
decked out for Easter Sunday,

helter-skelter, all-and-sundry.
The ancient cannibal
talked at length on Ice Age gneisses,
before drifting off to the rapist
played by that handsome actor with all the Emmys.
He'd been seen half-naked on a cruiser,

in a white Speed-Do. Her suit
had been panned from behind. Shot through a door
she appeared all alone, knee
deep in the mud. She showed him her real eyes,
not the ones she had in different
hues. His trousers began to swell,

no matter the swill
she forced down his throat. And he was hirsute.
He'd been told that before. She was indifferent,
staying warm and preferring the troubadour
love songs he could realize
from his lonely

days tying sheaths   of wheat. He was alone
then and now again. She's   a lone
soul whose anger seethes,   and accepts humor on loan.

Deep End

She bought the house for the cistern.
That and the megaphone
she found in the barn. Forever
he had said, his benign
smile still fresh on her mind. She'd awake
early and ignore the deplorable

hovels inflicted on the deportable.
He'd watched his sis turn
coat and run. They'd await
the fall when the megafauna
would have grown to be nine
feet, maybe ten. Scarlet fever

almost killed her. He'd dock
on the end, idle the twin Volvo
diesels, and prepare for the category
four. Two dinghies with an honor
guard could get them ashore. Hera,
their queen, and Ketchup,

their king, would catch up
with the guy in the docket.
He'd dare it for her. A
smooth chin on a wet vulva,
he'd been on her
and off her all week. When the cat left a gory

pile of puke near the bed her own quiet haven
was over. She turned the birch switch
into a Victorian rug beater
like she'd seen on TV. No one was upset.
She looked good in the veil
and had no use for a store. *Age*

before beauty, she'd heard him say, his storage
unit filled with Bibles and paintings of heaven.
He sold it all cheap. All to no avail.
Alas, the cut of her boot, the swish
of her skirt, something for them all to obsess
over. He'd tried to beat her

and her hatred deepened.   The Peace of
Paris (1783) had to depend   on the piece of
mischief at the deep end   of the page. She'd settle for pizza

Sonorous

Her idea of the holidays included ornaments.
If she had to blackmail
someone she would. Kidney
pie and the family around the sycamore.
Her lecture on botany
as it pertains to the sedimentary

rock right below them. They're a sedentary
lot, dependent on ointments
bought any
Thursday *if you wanted the black.* Male
nurses rubbed it into the sick. A more
blatant approach wouldn't do. Don't try to kid me.

The efforts to desegregate
the town were pitiful. A brain surgeon
could dance the flamenco
in a not too subtle
sort of way, and the catapult
had been calibrated in nanometers.

No matter.
It would all disintegrate.
The dog, not the cat, two poul-
try-eating sturgeons,
and the three guys in the sublet
needing more than one pink flamingo.

A second red whisker
in the soup and the cantaloupe,
spoiled, made her whimper
in a sonorous
whine he would nominate
for first prize. The new car, Es-

capade or Explorer, had been designed to caress
the driver. He'd whisk her
away. No more an inmate,
but they couldn't elope.
Their daughter or son or us,
all of us, played the wimp. Her

moments were calmest   when the odor
filled the room. The Communist   barked the order:
even the commonest   showed intense ardor.

Veneer

He promised Eden, an idyllic
place on a lake without tire
tracks. Far from Yale
where they could dress informally,
and always better
than anyone else. She'd play the bachelor,

and bring a batch a lor-
ry could drop at the door. He'd lick
it clean, and butter
up the guard at the corner tower,
a big guy formerly
known as a pastor. *Y'all*

need a green salad,
something simple, no hassle,
all part of a good meal. Lettuce, recent,
from near the bomb's fire
scorched the maniacs driving in reverse. I
saw the rats and the vermin

before, even before Vermont,
when we were together with Sal. Add
the dreams in Versailles,
and me being an asshole
en route to the Friday night bon fire
we would learn to resent.

They're whole veneer:
chamber music with an oboe,
two vocalists, a cello,
and several Objects
de Art, described in that acidic
tone. The argument turned secular,

though mostly circular,
and frequently unclear. Vermeer,
they loved. Though not Hasidic,
he was known to cry, *Oy vey*,
to the Ojibway
selling lime Jello

to the lion   tamer at Temple.
Both had the right to lie in   until ten. Pull
a fast one, you lyin'   cad, and collapse the tent pole.

Sediment

Steep the mountain, steeper the slope,
as were most chalets abroad.
He lived on the down low.
Late at night, Wednesdays,
his, no others, a basal
principle to decrease the duress.

Nine-inch heels and da dress
did the rest. The soap-
box car was her idea, the basil-
green hood a broad
span she found at Wendy's.
She'd learned to download

free coupons as a way out of the morass.
Avoid the one-time offer:
no quick vice-a-versa
with the pitiful pile on.
No salty sodomites
acting woodenly

toward women wittily
rejected in jest. *More ass*
he hollered from under the sheets. Ear mites
were another problem. When he got off her
she sneered. The last pilon
had moved. Her head felt in a vice. A verse,

a line, a stanza, sediment
from Vesuvius where a mummy
got up to belittle
an old guy with gravy
on his tie. In the chapel
she stood six-three.

The rafters, sixty
feet above, echoed what was said. It meant
the most for a chap. Pal
Joey, she called him. His mommy
buried near his father's grave. She
knew the gravestone would be little.

Jacked up on heroin
She was no heroine.
she'd seen the green heron

her odds wouldn't beat ten.
More muffled than beaten,
before she was ten.

Carloads

Edgar, Edwin, and Edward
met their cousin Arnold
and their uncle, King William I. Van
Cliburn won young, and Daniel
read the wall for signs of Whitney's Eli.
They met a guy named Ken next

door to the flat. Kenneth,
not Ken, though they called him Ed. Word
had it some no-account Yankee, ly-
ing through his teeth, said they weren't old
enough to fight. Dan, yell
as he might, didn't have a chance, and Ivan,

straight from the farm, knew of Christopher
Columbus and that's all. Carloads
of Frenchmen named Pierre
dropped to one knee and drew
a line in the sand. Michael,
an old friend, watched the hill cave in

around his cousin Kevin,
and swore to Christ, *O for
the love of God, give me an amp and a mic. All
I need right now is Carlos
Castaneda and Andrew
Yang, and a place to pee.* Air

quality could use attention, and some Jerry
Garcia would help. Brine
the chicken according to Chef Henry,
and re-cover the front yard in peat. Her-
shey bars all around. Straight from Alexander,
VA. Arrived pristine, without a blemish or bruise,

like the apples. Robert the Bruce
could have done better. No cherry-
picking for him. Alex's ex, and her
new husband Brian,
brought striped condoms and replaced the saltpeter,
with Morton's Kosher to brine the hen. Re-

garding the oven, William,   don't hesitate, do it.
Like your friend Willem   Dafoe with his new do. It
gave him free will. Limb-   for-limb, he'd perfer a donut.

Parakeets

She drank every night to pass out.
One-hundred-and-ten thousand
fans couldn't stop her, and the green salad
for lunch did naught. Adjust
to the rhythms, ignore the alarm,
and don't run more often

then you do now. She knew he'd jump offen
her soon. "Get your pass out,"
yelled the conductor, all arm
and no neck, interspersing his *thee* and *thine* with a *thou*. Send
the receipts in triplicate, and add just
the exact postage. My gal Sal. Add

it up. Memorize the Kaddish
and kneel. Salt Lake evaporated
and 800 parakeets
fluttered away. The "Preface"
to her new book made less noise.
She went with *Otto*,

for a title, the name of her first auto-
mobile, an Audi she drove for years. The cottage
bordered the sea. Her nose
and two toes were evacuated
in Desert Storm. Her preference,
Wordsworth's ballads and a pair of Keats's

odes over Shakespeare's sonnets. What is real
in the extreme doesn't matter in the extreme.
Their disagreement escalated into a quarrel,
inconsequential in the end. Independent
she might be, from five years at Tulane
where she studied Theoretical

Physics. A minor in Theatrical
Studies took her to Israel
where she learned to appreciate a two-lane
road of asphalt. The ex-stream
at the reservoir left an Indy pennant
for Foyt, dried up and torn. A squirrel

ran amok devouring radish   leaves, and a jogger
raced after rabbits.   Guillem's joglar
kept tune with a rabid   dog and an amateur juggler.

Ethereal

He believed that poetry
would right the world. Whatever
happened, whether footsore,
bed-ridden or ethereal,
he'd savor the applause,
riotous, and dissolve

the lead in his pipes. He would devolve
into history reading Poe. Try
as they might, the applesauce
was disgusting. Whatever
was in it made it taste like ether. Eel,
smoked by the Mohawk, measured a good foot. Sor-

orities were not his preference. The imitation
of femininity fogged his monocle,
and the new fillings
in his molars were more apparent
when he sighed. They showed
how the infantry, not the cavalry,

reenacted the charge of Calvary
in the war against decay. The intimation
that he owned, much less sold
the rights to Tati's *Mon Oncle*
through a parent
company with few feelings

was disproven by Carbon-
14 dating. The Marlboro
Man in a Jeep saw so-and-so and such-
and-such pretending to be human.
He doubted their legitimacy. Frankly,
the gals and their fellows

might know what follows
the exploding car bomb
near the Franklin
Institute. A slab of marble or
sandstone would do. For five years in Hunan,
he ate a sausage

with a wayfarer   plotting
after a communion wafer.   The potting
soil provided a waiver   for a gait all but plodding.

Canopies

He had heard of the promenade,
seen paintings and imagined the release
you would feel under canopies
striped blue and white. Additions,
they were, all of a sudden,
in the first quadrant

back, behind the quad. Rent
or his much-needed pomade?
The antidote would sadden
his mood. He'd be stalwart. Reverse
his only option. Addictions
had slowed him down. One can of peas

was all he could carry under his kilt.
Predictable Paddy,
his best buddy, could demonstrate
the perils of the addict.
Hip, though no Daddy-O,
this guy. Badminton,

his game. He was bad, mitten
on or mitten off. It was his. Killed
the bastards. He'd learned it from his daddy. Oh,
and his mother, too. Paddle
in one hand, a dick
in the other, he fought the demon straight

this time. Not the same cadaver.
He'd oil the new skillet,
put the chicken under
a brick, but first spray for raiding ants.
A light kohlrabi coleslaw
would go well, the kind with vinegar, not too sweet.

He could make it tout de suite,
throw it together. He'd been a cad. Ever-
and-never the cold sore
he rubbed on his chin. His skill at
the game and his radiance
were meant to undo

the delivery. A Spaceman,   wearing payes,
demanded his own space, man.   They will pay us
more if we get into space. Man-   on-the-moon? Try the *Payless*.

Aglow

She'd count the bullet points,
overwhelming in number. Richard Hugo
would have liked them, the way they invade
the space for the kingdom.
Baskets washed ashore
emerged from a silt

more brown than grey. Silk
Road or not, she heard the bullet, points
East, near a shore
she had walked once before. *You go,*
Girl. The king, dumb,
sent the message in vain.

Poor health
was a given.
If only they'd inform
her of her condition. *No way,*
the nurse told her with a smile all aglow.
She'd seen this before, local

farmers acting in loco
parentis, talking only of hell. The
snow, all a glow,
made the roof give in.
Only in Norway.
She'd leave next morning in form.

She'd show them whose shimmies
earned the rent, the sinecure
she'd hustled as *the morsel*
you've only dreamed of. Transparent,
she claimed, her *universal*
joint in a pink camisole

or the gray-and-white camo Saul
Bellow described. She preferred the chemise,
the one she had worn for Miss Universe. *I'll*
take it, she'd yelled, *a sin, a cure.*
Her trans parents
wanted no more. Sell

the ballet and the martial   arts to the cashier
looking to become a fire marshal.   Cash, ere
credit, worked in the marsh. Are   you blind? It's cashmere.

Cursive

Don't be reckless.
The bright red handkerchiefs
are best used by someone adept.
I know, I know. You're blessed.
What with one thing or another,
some other place, your parents,

my side of the pair. Rent's
going up. You'd been wreck-less
until you missed an otter
with a hanker'n', chief
among which was to cross the road. Bless Ed
for the swerve, a debt

your sense of mercy
can't repay. One saltine
for every hors d'oeuvre. The hard vest,
ribbed not fluted,
showed a cursive
logo with one starling

snarling, and startling
another. *Merci*
was the message, with *Curse if
you like*, embossed on the collar. Don't pour salt in
the wound or the flute. Ted
would tend to the harvest

and oversee publications.
He deserved a new pillow
or two, one for sleeping and another for riding,
as they did long ago
when the plains were overgrown,
and the Paleo-Indians arrived. The littoral

areas of the Great Lakes had a literal
meaning. When public actions
meant getting over, and grown-
ups scarfed a pill low
as if no one could see them, a goat
ate the only book in town, and writing

was no longer antedated.   One cup of black coffee
gave him *Anti! Dated!*   to paint on the coffin.
Older then antiquated,   the artisan needed more caffeine.

Bestill

The Rebs had surrendered,
in a holler more pastoral
than the pastures eunuchs
would have enjoyed. Art galleries
begged for his work, to edify
the masses. The play had two acts,

and one scene to axe
if it seemed too long. Surrounded,
they were, by a troop led by Ed. If I
relied on a past oral
exam he had it all: the calories,
by grams, percentages, and units.

Less than in smaller countries
with more adults and fewer children.
No TV or popular
culture, an underworld
where you had to be still.
The intensity of the familial

overwhelmed the familiar,
and forced them to count trees.
Ed waiverd. *Bestill*
my heart! The chilled wren,
the silk underwear,
and the Silver Poplars,

all illegal
no doubt. A snow blower
would have helped. The picket
line stayed strong with a Cornish
hen on the spit, and a curse
word yelled at Admissions.

Diesel emissions
alone would kill you. An ill eagle
tipped them off. The curves
too much in the snow. Blow or
shovel? They debated all day. The core niche
demanded a morning tweet. Get it

right this time, you're a senior   advisor. I'm President.
Smile when you call me Senor,   as I'm prescient
and have seen your   case. It lacks a precedent.

Neverland

When he heard the lion
roar, he knew where he was. Neverland!
He wouldn't have minded
if she hadn't try to fuck over
his next of kin. She'd visited the Italianate
Villa where she ate roasted cashews,

and tried not to sneeze. One more *achoo*
would be all he could take. Lines
of cops circled the house. The Italian ate
through it all. *Never-and*
Never, and *what the fuck, over*
the two replies he'd learned at the mine. Did

she wrap him in linen and herself in silk?
She had him, dead-to-rights. The circus
said *No* after the threat
of new polls made clear, *Reliques*
like Percy's would not do. He'd make a new headset,
designed for the rich to achieve

high-density resolution under the eaves.
The height made him sick,
and her, dead set
against the color, blew her circuits.
She burned the leeks
and lost the thread,

in a fashion not riotous
nor lame. The commonest
jockey knew a good satire
when he read one, even if the plot was superfluous,
and the verse no better than Jewel's.
There was a gap, hey,

when one believed in original sin and agape.
They were pacifists. *Riot, us?*
You want to know what's worse?
Them calling her a Communist.
How would that be super for us?
That and the bent axle and one sad tire.

They tried to plumb it,   the well. Bowered
by a peach and a plum, it   bowed
over the plummet.   They preferred boarded.

Up Here

She pretended to be asleep,
and after her wanderings
rest was imminent.
Her shoes were soaking wet
and her socks a mess, before she pilfered
the shack in the thicket.

Make it thick. It
won't stick otherwise. A sleep,
long and deep, and a pilsner
or two, had her wondering,
to wit,
what to make of him. And it,

the land, was terraced
by trained red necks
who appeared
now and then, relieved
by the conveniences
in the deal. Clearly,

somebody had read Creeley,
and knew him for the terrorist
he was. All those conveyances
round the world. Next
time, the relived
moment, up here,

would be more awesome.
The more graceless
proponent of the hammer and sickle
played tennis
with the original framer.
First editions

were all the rage, with small additions
to otherwise excellent work. Your flotsam
my jetsam, for the farmer
whose medical bracelet
gave him odds at tenish
to one. He'd been sick, ill

from the Amen   echoed by all.
Ah, men,   give them an awl
and a men's   group, all for the long haul.

Save Her

He'd read all of Defoe,
half of Fielding, and raised the ante
on finishing *Clarissa,* all nine volumes. Bodies
of baroque knowledge were his preference, and funding games
with no losers and less promise.
Sunday's ashes,

used to marked sheep, made asses
of them all. A fold
not a crease, his primary premise,
had been taught by the auntie
next door, in unison with her closest buddies.
All the fun-and-games

included at least one group in song,
and a tune known for its cacophony. The tone,
patriotic,
was belted out by a farm, er,
known to savor
the lewd and the vulgar.

The salad, made with bulgur,
added much to the so on
and so forth. He'd tried to save her.
Have her atone
for her sins. She wanted far more
then the patriarchal

system could allow. Ephemeral,
the English over here the Russians
over there, and Sophie
stuck in the middle. Further
along in his studies, the diction
introduced him to *svelt.*

His ego swelled,
as did a femoral
joint near the knee. The next thing he knew, addiction
was rife, and the Feds had to rush in
for there
was nothing else to do. So he

called Reggie,   talked testaments,
and interpreted red keys   to what testes meant
in Roethke.   That and the fresh mints.

Slowpoke

He collects antique first editions.
Nothing modern. His daughter prefers headphones.
The more expensive the better. What the girl achieves
will be remembered
when the cost of admission
reaches par. He's always been a slowpoke.

Used it to his advantage with his line about a slow poke
being just the ticket. The multiplications and additions,
the divisions and subtractions, shrank the ad. *Mission
Accomplished* a bit premature. His head, set
on an angle, let him re-member
the corpse, part-by-part. The eaves

still leak and will become
a deluge if a studious
janitor doesn't fix them today.
Tomorrow will be pressing it and Thursday
too late. The Covenant
in Time has finally

put a nail in the door. Finely
honed, the hornet and honeybee, come
what may, will serve a covert
operation to study us
tired, hungry, thirsty.
Brittle, too, day-

in-day out. They have to decrease
the load, hire a planter
or two, and make Tilly
the overseer. He sent it
overnight express. The bull's eye
was infected, and an adult

vet hard to find. A dulled
blade, even in degrees,
meant a missed bullseye
and the match. He'd plant her
on the other field, near the Senate
and the outlawed pesticides. Long

afterwards,   he'd sigh, *nigh*
unto an afterword.   The sign I
saw only after. Word   was, Mt. Sinai

Farce

He didn't know what to say. Utter
the wrong word and his life would be over. Her farts
were enough to kill ya. And the corral
next door, *where horseshit abounds,*
was no place to run amok.
He'd do the distance,

the one-two-shuffle, dis dance
and dat dance, while squeezing an udder
raw to the touch. Her muck-
splattered boots didn't help. The farce
went on. A pound
here, a pound there, he'd take it to her carrel

and weigh it. He'd twist one up in Barack
Obama rolling papers,
and keep a guard stationed
near the door. A Cassock,
he spit green secretions
in the pot of turnips
he shared with the nomads

living next door. No mad
officer would turn their barracks
upside down, no matter who might turn up.
She stayed tuned
for the broadcast on secret ions
transmitted from a cheap, wooden casket

made by an artisan named Sven,
and customized with ebony
handles. She'd tried catnip
with hash, and maligned
the manager of Staples.
Quinnipiac and Gallup

agreed. The horse couldn't gallop,
much less trot. They would fall short. Seven
weeks out, the stables
empty, and a boney-
assed cowgirl wanting to play *What's my line?*
Five winks in the AM and a cat nap

entered graciously,   more than once,
made him gratefully   express his wants.
Gracefully,   he tried not to wince.

In Toto

In total,
he threw out
the first hitter
and marooned
the next two on one
base. *Oh-I-oh*

became a hit, at least in Ohio,
where, in toto
no one, not one, none
of them, throughout
the land, wanted more room.
One hater

asked for the bread, the peacenik a baguette,
and some guy named Shorty
sang a tune
he learned inside. A long weekend
misremembered. Suppressed
by bold stances

the new stanzas
were designed to bag it,
not wrap it to go. Sue pressed
him on his height. Too short he
thought, and weakened
at the knees. They were attune,

the two of them, to the affairs
in the outlying
regions. Her aversion
to his time as a minstrel
gave an inflection
to the long emails

he sent to five females
he met years ago at the fair.
The rate of infection
skyrocketed outlining
a menstrual
inversion.

The yuppie   had learned to cock
and fire. It made him uppity,   what with the grandfather clock
and the new puppy.   If he could only learn how to caulk.

Hair's Breadth

She learned all she knew about asphalt
from the tar salesman she met near the exits.
He seemed nice, though loosely
wrapped with a layer of Clearasil
he applied with a furtiveness
she had not expected. His exploration

into everything had no expiration
date. It was her fault,
of that she was sure. She and the furtive nurse
who believed what exists
does so for a reason. He would clear a sill,
slap down his loose-leaf

notebook, and stack pens a hair's breadth
apart. He drew Greek colonades
in boring
reproductions, and in direct
opposition to the hearsay
that made for a briefer

rendition. The reefer
was fair, though it tasted like a hare's breath,
with hints of carrot and kale. It was all a heresy,
the prune juice and colon aids.
None of it had an indirect
effect on his borrowings,

money used to support his youngest daughter,
a young woman still using a Walkman.
She tried to evince
a clear answer. Did they plummet
down the bank in a plot
designed for a hollow scene

or was it for the closing shot of the Holocene?
They had needed to see a doctor,
that and a willingness to applaud
with gusto. When they decided to walk, man,
they left him to plumb it,
alone. Clear evidence

of Yahweh   in Auden?
Have it your way.   She awed 'em
with one *Rah Yay*   and her ode to autumn.

Outlawed

They had plenty of A positive, and no type Os.
It's what the state allowed.
The doctors working on the harlot
let us
pray. The dog fights and cat attacks
remained undeserved.

It was the usual underserved.
They wrote well, but the typos
crimped cataracts
when read aloud.
They wouldn't know arugula from lettuce,
though they'd eat a lot

of either if given the chance. The outcry
almost absolved
the defection of the muse.
Inspiration, a new réflex
they learned from the Tartars,
the winners

all winter
both inside and out. Cry-
ing about a little tartar
doesn't work the abs. All
commotion reflected
today was made to amuse

the crowd protesting out loud.
Only a goof
would see a pair of parasites
and mistake
them for a herd on a range.
How big is the planet?

And who's going to plan it?
With everything outlawed
who can arrange
anything? And a way to go? Of
the two hits and a miss, Steak
Hoolihan had the answers. From a pair of sights

in his carry-on   to the light and
water he'd carry on,   he'd light in
to the carrion   left behind to enlighten.

NOTES

My recollection of the sources for found poems in this book varies from knowing not only the poet but the poem or line or direct quote to remembering only the poet or the poem. Here's what I recall about how they began:

"A Third Love Note to Alice" (Gertrude Stein)

"This Makes for Peace!" (Joan Murray)

"Dirty Face, Ripple and Wild" (from a letter Robert Creeley wrote to Charles Olson in Vol. III of *The Collected Correspondence*)

"Others" (Edna St. Vincent Millay)

"Ballycurragh" (the James Joyce Tower & Museum, maybe)

"Voyage VII" (a collage of lines by Walt Whitman, Langston Hughes, Hart Crane, and others I can't recollect)

"An Epitaph for Mortal Folk" (*Words in Air: The Complete Correspondence Between Elizabeth Bishop and Robert Lowell*)

"To the Modernists: A Cento" (see below for complete annotation)

"Couplets Concerning Margaret" (Donald Justice's "Couplets Concerning Time" and several others of his poems in couplets)

"Al's Vacation" (Lorine Niedecker's "North Central" and the Margot Peters biography, *Lorine Niedecker: A Poet's Life*)

"Variations on a Line from Frost" (*The Letters of Robert Frost, volume I, 1886 – 1920*)

"Advice for a Young Poet" (the Langdon Hammer biography, *James Merrill: Life and Art*).

"To the Modernists: A Cento" includes lines from the following poets: Ezra Pound (lines 1and 4); T. S. Eliot (lines 3, 6, 7, 19 & 20); Wallace Stevens (lines 2, 12, 22, 28, 32 & 36); William Carlos Williams (lines 8, 9, 16, 23, 30 & 31); Robert Frost (lines 5, 10, 17, 18 & 39); Gertrude Stein (lines 21 & 25); Edwin Arlington Robinson (lines 11 & 14); Edna St. Vincent Millay (line 13); Claude McKay (line 15); Hilda Doolittle [HD] (lines 24, 27 & 33); Marianne Moore (line 26); William Butler Yeats (line 29); John Crowe Ransom (lines 34 & 38); and Mina Loy (lines 35, 37 & 40). I wanted to put the answers at the bottom of the page, upside down, in smaller print so the reader could approach it like a quiz with points. 40 points = A+.

"Part Two: Burlesques": These nonce poems merge the sestina with an expanded version of the homonym, both of which are being burlesqued. I use the rhyme scheme of the sestina, but replace rhyming words with phrases that in many cases initiate the homonym. For the concluding stanza, I rely on the Anglo-Saxon line that breaks in the middle, and rhymes or alliterates, internally. Unlike the traditional Anglo-Saxon line that tended to be in couplets, my concluding stanza is a tercet with the rhyme coming at the break in the line and at the end of the line.

ABOUT THE AUTHOR

Peter F. Murphy grew up on the St. Lawrence River in Alexandria Bay, NY, the Heart of the Thousand Islands, where he learned to ice fish and shoot pool. His poems have appeared in the *Birmingham Poetry Review, New Madrid, The Café Review, Neologism Poetry Journal*, and three chapbook anthologies. In 2009, and again in 2013, Murphy attended the Sewanee Writer's Conference at The University of the South. His chapbook, *A Map of Three Continents*, was published in 2020 by Moonstone Press. In addition to his poetry, Murphy's critical work includes *Studs, Tools, and the Family Jewels: Metaphors Men Live By; Fictions of Masculinity;* and *Feminism and Masculinities* (a volume in the Oxford Readings in Feminism series). His essays and reviews have been published in, among other journals, *The Review of Contemporary Fiction, Twentieth Century Literature, Modern Fiction Studies, College Literature, Signs,* and *Feminist Studies*. He lives with his wife in Philadelphia, PA.

He can be contacted at: pmurphy@murraystate.edu.

Made in the USA
Middletown, DE
22 January 2022